Fun Things ~~to Do in~~

Retirement

Affordable Activities that Will Create a Fun and Fulfilling Retirement and Enrich your Life!

Robert Cavaliere

Table of contents

Introduction

It is said that "retirement is not the end of the road; it is the beginning of the open highway," and I completely second that. The two years before my retirement, I used to see it as some scary phase of life that I just had to go through. But it wasn't like that at all; I never enjoyed myself as much as I started enjoying after my retirement; it was like reconnecting to my true self. I did everything that was on my bucket list, and I set up my own little online shop, which is still growing today. Life today is now full of satisfaction, peace and contentment. With a positive approach towards the whole retirement phase, you can turn the tables around and live a financially stable and happy life with your loved ones. It just needs some effort and planning on our part to prepare for what is coming ahead of us. I recommend everyone start planning their post-retirement life at least two years before retirement. Before retirement, most people only look for financial security, and they take all the measures to save for themselves and their families as much as they can; while that is an important part of planning, it is not the only thing that should be of concern. How you will spend your savings and time after retirement must be another matter of grave concern. Sitting idle all day at home might sound amazing when you are working, but after a week or two of retirement, not doing anything might drive you crazy. Yes, this has happened to me before, and it was so depressing that it almost sent me into a depressive state. The only way to fight boredom is to find yourself some constructive, useful and soulful activity. In this short guidebook, I have compiled all the possible ways you can spend your time after retirement. So if you are soon to be retiring or retired already, this list of activities is a must-to-read; maybe you will find your true calling there, just like I did!

What Is Retirement?

It is the time of your life when you are officially free from the workforce and are old enough to live on the pension, funds or any other retirement program. The criterion for retirement is different in every country, and the pension policies vary from organization to organization. In the US and many other countries worldwide, the average retirement age is 65 years. The early retirement age is almost 60-62 years. The age limitation varies with different cases. People manage their post-retirement lifestyle depending on what financial securities your state or country offers for retirees. Life after retirement changes for good, and suddenly a person who was previously working 8-12 hours a day gets all the free time in the world. Without work, most people lose their sense of usefulness and purpose, which may lead to depression. It is, therefore, important to actively prepare for this phase of life and to see it as a new chapter of your life, not the final one.

Why Retirement Is Important?

People around the world have mixed feelings about the word retirement; some anticipate it, whereas some find it scary. Well, in my opinion, retirement comes with a set of advantages, so much so that people have started going for early retirement these days. You can concentrate on improving your quality of life if you switch too early retirement. Age 65 was traditionally seen as the starting point for retirement for many years. Some Americans have grown to find the concept of retiring early quite appealing in recent years. Due to the pandemic and economic unpredictability, some businesses have decided to retire personnel, usually offering incentives in exchange. If you are considering retiring in your 40s or 50s, you should carefully consider this life-altering option. Although leaving a job you don't enjoy behind could be appealing, there are also financial and social factors to take into account. In the end, the option to leave your job in the past has some excellent benefits and some issues that you will need to resolve. Early retirement has benefits, including:

- Freedom from workspace limitations: After retirement, you can finally focus on your dream business or investment plan or take up a hobby you must have neglected.
- Time to engage in activities: After retirement, you can finally focus on the sport, arts or crafts you like.
- A good boost to one's well-being: with no work pressure, your health actually improves after retirement. You can work on your diet and join a gym to stay healthy as well as fit.
- The freedom to decide on more work

Over the past few decades, a significant shift has occurred in how people see retirement. We all have considerably higher expectations for life after work than previous generations did. A few of the many things we might have on our minds include traveling the world, visiting fascinating new locations, spending time with the family, and engaging in hobbies. We anticipate extended retirement planning as the retirement age restriction in the private and public sectors decreases day by day. That calls for thoughtful planning in order to support the lifestyle you desire after retirement.

However, with costs rising and a global economic situation in turmoil, everyone's dream retirement life looks improbable

How To Manage Finances

The only thing that stops you from having a peaceful and happy retirement life is bad financial status. You may get a lot of advice about saving your money and assets for the retirement days, but no one emphasizes enough the importance of managing finances once you are retired. While it seems like most financial advice is focused on helping you save money for retirement, whether you are retiring early or on schedule, very little of it seems to be concerned with helping you manage that money. No matter how much money you save during your work life, it cannot last forever if you are not smart about spending it at the right time and right place. Prudent money management in retirement is essential to guaranteeing that your nest egg can last you through your golden years without requiring you to cut back on expenses or possibly unretire. You will have to take all the necessary steps to keep your reserves full with extra savings to spend on your leisure activities. Every financial decision you make should be carefully calculated to ensure that you are safeguarding your future because you won't have the security of a career to support your cash. Only after managing your finances and drawing out a complete financial plan can you decide which activities you can afford to enjoy during this phase of life. To help you better manage your funds, the following are some suggestions from financial professionals.

Don't Let Your Money Expire

Outliving your salary is the main concern while managing your finances throughout retirement. You will need enough money to cover your basic demands without having to go back to work later on or take more severe measures. No matter how much money you have saved up for retirement, you still need to prepare ahead. When it comes to this issue, you cannot be too careful. Figuring out how to draw money from your investment portfolio to sustain you in retirement today while allowing for growth to bolster your income in the future presents a difficulty for managing money in retirement.

If you plan to retire early, you will need to make sure you have readily accessible assets in addition to those in retirement accounts like an IRA or 401(k) to draw from (k). Many tax-advantaged retirement plans won't permit withdrawals until you reach age 59 1/2 (at least not without a penalty). If you're planning to retire early, you'll need to put money aside to cover the time before when you stop working and once you can begin utilizing your Social Security benefits and retirement savings, which you may get at age 62, although your monthly allowance check will be decreased. Since you won't be eligible for Medicare until you are 65, you will also need to consider your medical expenses. Retirement can be challenging when all of these factors are considered, but smart planning will assist.

Set Up A Budget

How much you spend will greatly impact how long your money lasts. A Ford budget won't get you very far if you prefer a Ferrari. To begin with, it's crucial to anticipate your retirement spending so you may adjust your spending plan to accommodate your needs and wants.:

→ Do you still owe money on your house's mortgage?

→ When you retire, do you want to go traveling?

→ Do you intend to keep your spending to a minimum?

→ Can you cut back on your expenditures until you can establish alternative income sources.

→ With more leisure time, would your spending increase?

→ During any gap years, how will you pay for health insurance?

→ Can you relocate to a top retirement location while saving money?

Determining your resources can help you achieve your goals; you will need to have a solid estimate of how much you will spend. You must also take care to avoid spending during your early retirement from derailing your future ambitions. If you run out of resources quickly, you might have to make drastic cuts later on in order to get by. Or it might entail returning to work later and making far less money than you can today. You should be as honest as you can at this point and then add extra expenditures for the unanticipated expenses that always seem to arise. You can spend more flexibility later if you start out with more conservative estimations.

Assets Analysis

You should know how much money you have in your taxable brokerage accounts, bank accounts, and any other areas where money is readily available. You can start drawing Social Security if you are older than 62 and can access retirement assets with no penalty if you are older than 59 1/2 years old. However, you should carefully consider when it is ideal to use that money source. Many early retirees will be unable or unwilling to tap into their retirement assets, despite the fact that there are a few options. If you reach the age of

55 and have already left the employer where the 401(k) is held, you can either make a withdrawal or a series of equal quarterly installments. If you are taking a retirement, taking money out of your retirement account should only be done as a last resort. You must determine how long your assets will last until you may access extra income based on your budget.

It would be best to consider your entire retirement, not the time until additional money comes in. You should also consider how much money you should take out of the account at first. The "4% rule" is commonly recommended by experts. You should only take out 4% of your retirement assets. Your investments have a chance to increase in value in subsequent years if you leave enough in the account. You will need long-term growth to lessen the damaging consequences of inflation on your holdings.

Your money can last longer for quite some time at a withdrawal rate of 4 percent, but many financial experts today believe that this amount may be excessive, given the low returns on fixed-income instruments like bonds. So some consultants advise retirees to withdraw no more than 3%

from their portfolios. These additional withdrawal techniques could make your retirement funds last longer.

However, you should certainly proceed with particular caution when retiring. Early in retirement, a minor error could significantly impact the remainder of your years of retirement. Therefore, choosing a lower withdrawal rate will be more prudent and allow you more flexibility in the future.

Maintain A Balanced Portfolio

If you are preparing for retirement, you will need to manage your financial portfolio carefully to ensure that you have money for both now and tomorrow. You want to keep a high level of safety in your investments, and you don't want to have to sell high-return assets like stocks when their value declines. In the past, transferring funds from equities to bonds was simpler, and you could take advantage of a reliable and secure income source. Unfortunately, it is more difficult to generate adequate, stable income now due to the relatively low bond yields. Due to rising interest rates, bonds are no longer as secure as they once were for bondholders, making them less appealing to investors.

Financial advisors have historically used the "Rule of 100" to assist investors in making decisions regarding how much of their portfolio to allocate to bonds and how much to equities. You deduct your age from 100 to determine the ideal stock allocation in your portfolio to determine how aggressive it should be.

For example, if you are 55 years old, the guideline recommends that you hold 55 % in bonds and 45% of your stock's portfolio. According to the norm, you should invest 35% of your portfolio in equities if you are 65 years old. So your portfolio grows more safely as you become older. However, given the low bond yield, it may make sense to allocate more money to equities using the Rule of 120, as some experts suggest. To determine your ideal stock allocation, deduct your age from 120. According to the updated guideline, if you were 55, 65 percent of your assets should be invested in equities. With a longer retirement, you are more likely to require the additional growth provided by this greater allocation, which would provide you with more growth over time.

Managing your financial portfolio is not easy, and you would need to invest more of your time and planning skills. And if you lack the will and expertise to do so, then you can always take someone else's help. First, you could collaborate with a financial counselor who can perform that laborious task on your behalf. To get the greatest counsel for your case, make sure you deal with a fee-only advisor who you pay.

Manage Accounts.

You should make use of your tax-advantaged retirement accounts to their full potential. You will be better off if you allow them to compound for a longer period without having to pay tax on the gains. Financial gurus advise that you take funds from your accounts in the following order: tax-deferred accounts should be withdrawn first, then taxable accounts, to allow those special accounts to develop. Premature retirement savings should be drawn primarily from taxable accounts, considering that tax-advantaged retirement accounts have greater value, are more hard to acquire, and are subject to penalties if withdrawn until retirement age is reached. It makes sense to spend taxable funds first when you can, even when it comes time to withdraw money from your retirement accounts.

Control Your Spending

You will need to maintain your portfolio throughout time, as well as make sure that your daily financial management is in order. You may avoid the necessity to sell once the stock market is falling and retain your stock portfolio long-term growth by efficiently managing your portfolio. Having an emergency fund with at least one year's worth of expenses in cash is essential to accomplishing this. If the market is down, you won't have to sell into it, and you will have the assurance that your money is always available. Depending on how much you spend, some planners even suggest having at least two years' worth of expenses or more. Numerous experts advise their customers to categorize their finances into three categories:

Short-Term expenses: It is possible to convert your money and other short-term fixed income assets into cash with no or little loss of principal. To get the most out of your investments, move them to the highest-yielding accounts possible. Your reserves enable you to continue making long-term investments.

Intermediate-term expenses: This category includes assets that you will require between three and seven years from now. These investments could have a slight safety bias, but given the long time horizon, you could also include growth assets like stocks.

Long-term: expenses: You invest your money in riskier, higher-yielding assets like equities in this bucket because you won't need to access them for seven years or more. These investments have more time to recover from market fluctuations and continue to perform well due to the extended time horizon. Instead of shooting for the stars, this strategy aims to give investors a good chance of making significant long-term gains.

When you deplete it, you will need to add cash from your other buckets to your cash reserve. You can transfer money from other accounts to your cash reserve if it comes from fixed-income assets or dividend equities. However, you can rebalance your portfolio while also reaping long-term capital gains.

As an example, if a stock fund or stock has exceeded the rest of your portfolio, you may take some of that gain and shift it to a more stable asset that can provide income or even cash. Search for instances where your assets have drastically exceeded and are far from your intended allocation rather than trying to time when you do this. It's imperative to keep safety in mind while you handle your money, both in the long and near term. Even though it can seem secure to put all of your assets in short-term income investments, you will eventually lose money due to inflation. However, if you need to use that money immediately, you can't invest all of it in equities.

Ways To Achieve A Happy Retirement

Depending upon how you handle your retirement phase, this phase of life can be really fun, or it can really be depressing. You have many options to forge your own course as you enter the retired period of life. There are a slew of options available to help you prepare for a decent retirement. There are strategies to maximize your retirement at every stage, even though health circumstances and living arrangements can vary. Consider these pieces of advice to have a happy retirement:

New Objectives

During your working years, you may have had specific goals, like aiming for a promotion or reaching a certain number of years of employment. Achieving those goals is still possible in retirement, and they often serve to drive you to new limits. You can set new goals and objectives for this new phase of life. Think of it as another dawn and set targets like checking off your bucket list, traveling, completing a project or setting up a business. Setting goals and objectives will help you regain a sense of purpose.

Keep To Your Means

If you haven't previously done so, now may be the time to put together a retirement budget. Our happiness during retirement is jeopardized when our financial stability is threatened. You would be on your road to a pleasant retirement if you spent less than you made your entire life. Make sure that you have an emergency fund and a plan in place to pay off any outstanding debts so that unforeseen events won't result in financial instability.

Stay Socially Connected

Isolating yourself is never good for retirees. You need to connect with those who are in the same situation as you. Interacting with them is great for your mind. You can learn new things and get inspired to do more in life than just sitting at home and watching television. Look for activities in your region to engage in social contact if you aren't already a member of an organization or a regular social gathering club.

Engage In Brain Games

There are many ways to practice your mental skills daily, from reading books to using apps and online games. Go out and resolve a challenging issue. If you enjoy assisting others in learning, you can search for a volunteer position or part-time work where you might spend a few hours a week tutoring children. Playing weekly card games or acquiring new talent, like the piano or a foreign language, are two other methods to stay stimulated. =

Mend and Renew Relationships

Searching for old friends and acquaintances could be beneficial if you still reside in the same region where you attended high school or college. Your shared interests or desire to meet a new acquaintance might lead to an interesting conversation with you. Seek out your relatives and be prepared to resolve any issues from the past that may have harmed your relationship. Family ties are crucial, and even shaky ones may sometimes be repaired.

Take on Work

After leaving a career, there are many ways to remain active and happy. However, we don't have to shun all forms of work or service in our retirement because it will make life easier and less hectic for you. Find a job that makes you proud, and that has inherent value to you. You might provide multiple times per week care for your grandchildren, serve as a volunteer at your church, or look after elderly friends who want your help. Keep your options open, so you can take that trip you've always wanted to take, sleep in some mornings, and get more rest than you have previously.

Ask For Help

Retirement often offers a period of independence and adaptability. It could be pleasurable at first to maintain your home and your new way of life. It might be time to call out if you get to the point where you can no longer handle things on your own. Family members could deliver groceries to you and mow your lawn. Housework and other errands that you cannot perform can be taken care of by caregivers. By asking for help, you may be able to maintain your independence, stay in your home, and engage in the activities you enjoy.

Free Yourself

Freeing yourself from the unwanted anxiety, pressures, and the idea of losing purpose in life after retirement is a struggle and a retiree goes through this process in phases. Most retirees won't have a clear-cut action plan to follow immediately; instead, they will likely go through a severe identity crisis. It is important to know what is likely to happen to you when you retire so that you can better prepare your mind for it. Usually, after finishing your primary full-time job, you will go through a honeymoon period that lasts for less than a year. The honeymoon stage is liberating, novel, and thrilling since you are free from a job and a life of obligation. But then comes the disenchantment stage. You feel exhausted and attempt to spend your free time with activities suggested by friends and family, but deep down, you aren't truly satisfied.

In the reorientation stage, you discontinue those activities you initially liked and ended up disliking them. You become aware of the necessity to assess your life again and decide what's best. Most individuals only then begin to realize that gaining clarity might be advantageous. You fully accept your status as a retiree and settle into a routine during the stability period. It's critical that you accept an identity that properly reflects your core principles by the time you reach the stability stage. Otherwise, you risk missing out on your true purpose, ambitions, and dreams for your life after retirement and becoming more prone to despair and solitude. To clearly see the life you want, you must take some time to reflect on yourself. Finding that insight will need a genuine commitment to actively listening from within, which is no small task and much easier said than done.

Kinds Of Retirement Activities

There are endless ways to spend your post-retirement time on activities that you can actually enjoy. You may connect with your mind and listen to your heart to discover what it really desires. It can be a lucrative business that you can invest in, or it can be something as simple as collecting your favorite mineral rocks, or you can carry out multiple activities simultaneously. In other words, the steering is in your hands; with your finances managed, you can start with any of the following activities. Just let your inner creativity flow and see where it takes you.

Sport

When you get older, you don't need to exercise as much, right? – Well, that is Wrong. Many people believe that as we age, we need less exercise. However, it's true that maintaining muscular and bone strength as we age is essential to prevent our bodies from becoming weak and feeble. Many people put their health at risk as they age by not exercising. So Let's be smart about and treat our bodies with wisdom and live up to the phrase "old and wise." There is no harm in keeping yourself smart, active and occupied simultaneously. You can pick up some sports for your daily routine and dedicate some days to that sport. Following are some good options:

Bowling

It is a decent, albeit outdated, one. It fulfills all the requirements: it is competitive, social, active, and therapeutic. Bowls is a fantastic sport to get involved in, and there are numerous clubs to join in all parts of the world.

Cycling

Cycling is a terrific activity to get you back into exercising because it is far easier on the joints than jogging, according to studies that show that regular exercise can lower the risk of dementia. It's a terrific way to stay fit, whether you ride a bike at the gym or go outside and breathe the fresh air. You might also become a bike club member and meet some new people there. The advantage of cycling is that you can do it anywhere, whether you are living in the mountains, in the city, suburbs or near the sea.

Golf

Scenic, serene greenery surrounded by the outdoors is what comes to mind when I think of gold. Why wouldn't you pick golf as a kind of a healthy activity? The technique is the key to this soothing activity, making it ideal for individuals who prefer competition without pressure. But don't let this leisurely game mislead you; it may help you burn more calories than visiting the gym. An 18-hole course can be walked around in a game, and up to 1500 calories can be burned. It's a great way to meet new people, expand your social circle, and keep active all at the same time. You can start by getting a golf club membership or asking your friends around to find a good place to golf.

Swimming

A wonderful, all-body workout is swimming. The water supports the body's weight; there is less impact on the joints, thus reducing the chance of pain for people with arthritis. It is a calming activity that can help you unwind and get a good night's sleep, in addition to strengthening and conditioning your muscles. And if swimming isn't something that attracts you, then you can try out a variety of other water sports, like water polo and aqua aerobics.

Tennis

Tennis is for you if you enjoy a little rivalry! Tennis is both a fantastic physical workout and a ton of fun. It will also raise your bodily health; if you play competitively, you need to be alert and tactical, giving your brain a workout. It will also improve your overall health, strength, and agility. As you play hard and have fun, your stress levels will decrease. You're less likely to suffer from anxiety and sadness if you play a sport you're passionate about.

Education

Retirement is perhaps the perfect time for you to pursue a degree or study more about a subject you've always been interested in. Although the age criteria vary, every state provides opportunities for retirees to receive free or significantly reduced college tuition. Across the state, colleges and universities offer programs created for people over 50. There are numerous free ways to broaden your mind. Join online classes, watch some TED talks or podcasts, or you can visit seminars or workshops. Visit a museum or science center; many provide free admission to seniors or on specific days. Consider instead massive open online courses (MOOCs), which provide free college-level programs in a variety of areas, including psychology, web design, music, game development, chemistry, economics, art, communication, and many more. Besides learning from an institute, there are plenty of other ways to work in education:

Become A Mentor:

Do you want to teach others what you know? There are numerous mentorship programs out there that are constantly looking for volunteers. This is how to serve your community and put your free time to good use. You can mentor online or join an institute for this purpose. A freelance mentorship is also a great option; you can charge people for classes as well if you want to earn for yourself.

Read

Everyone would like to read more, just like they would like to exercise more. Maybe there are certain books you've always wanted to read. Or you could just start by searching online for the top 25 novels published in the previous 25 years. Regardless, reading is a satisfying habit that will keep your mind in shape.

Learn A Second Language

Even if you don't travel the world in retirement, picking up a new language is a good pastime for retirees, and it may even slow the aging process. There are several free language courses available online on YouTube; you can start from there without paying a penny to anyone. Practice and master one language, then move to the next.

Music

Music feeds the soul and can make one great activity for your post-retirement period if you learn to play an instrument or simply listen to good music. Listening completely depends on your preference and taste in music, so that I won't advise you on that, but I can recommend some techniques and tips for playing music. When you're retired, consider training up a musical instrument to help sharpen your mind and lift your spirits. You can find YouTube tutorials on playing a certain instrument, buying books, reading articles or finding a teacher with previous experience instructing music. Ask your teacher whether they'd be available to come to your house if that's more convenient for you. Look for someone professional who has a solid reputation in the community. Finding an instructor with a cheerful and upbeat disposition is crucial because they will keep you engaged and enthused about your instrument. Here are two of the instruments that are super easy to learn, and you can learn them to play at home as well.

Piano

Particularly the piano has provided an unrivaled avenue for individuals looking for solace, freedom of expression, and pure delight. A keyboard is used to play the 88 keys on the modern piano, which has 36 black keys and 52 white keys altogether. The piano was created for use in many different genres of music, including classical, jazz, traditional, and popular, in the year 1700. It is sometimes regarded as the ideal instrument to learn how to play because of its great versatility, large dynamic range, and wide range. Piano players of all ages can benefit physically and physiologically from the unique workout that is piano playing. You can learn to focus, persevere, and communicate your emotions. It will improve your focus and memory while fostering better fine motor skills and concentration. Learning this musical instrument is also a very soothing and pleasant experience. It has been demonstrated that practicing the piano significantly reduces tension and offers several chances to boost self-esteem.

Violin

Among the string instruments, the violin stands out as the tiniest and loudest. The violin is a four-stringed instrument that is played by sweeping a bow across the strings. Jazz, country, metal, and folk music are just a few of the many musical genres in which violins are essential instruments. Learning to play the violin offers many advantages, including enhancing discipline, coordination, and focus. More than almost any other musical instrument, the violin calls for perfect posture. Maintaining your body and violin in the appropriate position for long periods requires strength and balance. The upper arm and shoulder muscles must be incredibly strong to play the violin. In fact, practicing the violin is similar to doing an upper-body workout in the gym. The violin is the ultimate multi-tasking instrument since playing it enhances your physical strength, hand-eye coordination, and agility.

Dancing

Dance is a fun way to move your body and make it active and healthy. I have seen many retirees around me who started dancing after 50 and have been doing it since. The great thing about dancing is that you can try any style, whether it is ballroom dancing, tango, Zumba, salsa, or simply the "clearinghouse" boogie. Whatever you decide, you will enjoy the advantages of a fantastic workout. Your heart and lungs will thank you for it, your coordination, agility, and flexibility will all improve, and you will generally be stronger and happier as a result.

Exercise is important for living a healthy lifestyle and offers people from all walks of life several important advantages. As a result of this, it's critical that both you and your beloved one adjust the level of exercise and activity to suit their individual requirements. Most of the time, it's ideal for adding easy and enjoyable exercise regimens for older adults. The following dance exercises are great to try:

- Jazz dancing
- Salsa dancing
- Line dancing
- Waltz
- Tap dancing
- Ballet
- Seated dancing or chair aerobics

I recommend enrolling in adult dancing classes or joining a group. In this way, you will stay indulged in this activity. There are Zumba schools that you can join to start your dance routine. While dancing to the beats of flamenco, salsa, and merengue, Zumba is popular because it seems much like a dance party rather a workout. Anyone may join a Zumba class; you do not even have to be a professional dancer to participate. Zumba is all about dancing to music and having fun without any requirement for rhythm.

Writing

By the time you retire, you have enough experiences, stories and pearls of wisdom that you can share with others. Many retirees like writing plays, novels, cookbooks, memoirs, poems, and how-to manuals. You may create a blog on traveling, cooking, listening to music, or retirement in general. Or you might just write for yourself. It is a fantastic approach to writing memories, reducing stress, and processing emotions by keeping a personal diary. Writing can be lucrative if you write for a website, blog, or advertising company. Listed below are a few of possibilities that you should definitely try:

Get Paid For Copywriting:

It is not required to be a writer in order to write copy. Many websites, such as LinkedIn, Codify, Reblogger, or Indeed, provide writing jobs where you can earn money. You may search for editing, copywriting, and other creative jobs on Upwork. The Dos and Don'ts of copywriting and how to do it are all available on the internet; you can read into the details and start practicing your skills as a copywriter. Write a few good samples, and share them with potential clients to start working. Web content is another domain that you can work in. It is more contemporary, and it keeps you engaged. You can run your own website and produce content for it.

Think About Blogging

Is it possible to actually make money by blogging? Yes! In fact, some people earn staggering sums of money, and for a large number of people, it serves as their sole source of income. Typically, making money requires a lot of dedication and perseverance; it rarely happens quickly. Can it still be considered work if you choose a subject you find interesting to talk about? It is a fun way to work. By blogging, you can share your expertise, routine or content about anything you like with people and when you interact with them online.

Collecting

Collecting is a satisfying activity that can be lucrative if you collect valuable items. It is only a matter of your interest; some people collect stamps, some old coins and some rocks etc. There are countless different things you can collect. Here are a few things that elderly and young guys have accumulated over the years. Due to the fact that new products aren't rare or unique, collecting vintage and antique items is virtually always more enjoyable (and lucrative). Start some research if something interests you, then dive in!

Numismatic

The coin collection is an engaging activity, and it has a long history that dates back to the era of kings like Caesar Augustus. To encourage commercial agreements, it is said that Augustus gathered coins of all kinds from various nations and delivered them as gifts to other foreign leaders. In order to ascertain the relative rarity of the coins they study, modern numismatics investigates the creation and usage of money, medals, and currencies from the 17th century onward. The variants, mintage totals, mint-made mistakes, and social, political, and economic aspects of coin production are also of interest to researchers, and you can learn all about them by buying books and reading articles online.

The internet and other contemporary communication tools have made it easier to explore the history of coins and exchange knowledge with other researchers, facilitating the study of coinage in the modern era. Coin enthusiasts and scholars have founded regional coin organizations and societies to share information and global history. Numismatists can now easily browse through historical coin study materials thanks to the internet. You can display your coin collecting in a hard book or on a display board; then, you can enter the circa, the notes and details about those coins.

Wine Collection

Like baseball cards, vehicles, and artwork, wine has well-established histories, vintages, and tiers of value. Due to their suitability for collection, rare wines are one of the most coveted items on the market. A sub-economy of the ultra-rare can take center stage, and prices can appear ridiculous to outsiders, like with many high-end collectibles. But wine bottles can be sold at a very high price so that you can collect old bottles of champagne and wine in your cellar.

Cards Collection

Playing card collections may be an extremely lucrative pastime. I've had a fascination for it for a long time, and I still enjoy spending time adding to my collection. Do you know that card collection is so popular that now the hobby is celebrated on a playing card collection day? One of the earliest kinds of portable art, National Playing Card Collection Day, honors the collection of playing cards (circa the 1200s). Playing cards are actual galleries of inspiration and art, displaying and explaining to the public an artist's intentions while recording the moment's cultural values. By gathering these works of art, we may create galleries that can be used to symbolize various historical junctures. This is a day to recognize collectors and display their wares to the public. You can join online and offline groups of card collectors and share your collection with others. These collections can be considered extensions of the collectors themselves as they reflect your beliefs.

In addition to this, there are a number of other items that you may collect:

- Art
- Autographs
- Badges
- Books
- Board games
- Business cards
- Campaign buttons
- Casino chips
- Cigar bands
- Challenge coins
- Cigar boxes
- Coin banks
- Clocks
- Coins
- Comics
- Cologne bottles
- Die-cast
- Drink coasters
- Foreign money

- Fishing lures
- Fountain pens
- Fossils
- Guns
- Hats
- Journals
- Keys
- Keychains
- License plates
- Lunch boxes
- Lighters
- Maps/globes
- Magazines
- Marbles
- Matchbooks
- Musical instruments
- Mugs
- Neckties/bowties
- Oil cans
- Patches
- Playing cards
- Photographs
- Pocket Knives
- Postcards
- Posters
- Records
- Smoking pipes
- Souvenir spoons
- Sports cards
- Tools
- Toys
- Stamps
- Watches

The excitement of the search and the quest is a big part of collecting that keeps you engaged. You can be out and about looking for the next item to add to your collection on the weekends instead of sitting on your butt watching movies. Visit an antique shop at your own pace. Only the most expensive and cherished goods will be visible if you quickly search the shelves and display cases. You will likely unearth some goodies if you search through every box and case.

Performing

Performing is one of the most satisfying activities you can try for yourself if you ever dream of acting. Opting for the performing arts will require some extra effort and lots of determination, along with some natural talent for it. Remember that you are only trying it to satisfy yourself; it does not have to be a big hit or sale. Joining theater groups and learning to act with others can be a good start. With this experience, you will not only enjoy learning acting and singing, but you will also get to interact and socialize with so many new people on a daily basis. So it is a win-win for you.

From theater, you can drift to musical theater and opera as well. You have a number of alternatives to pick from:

- Theater
- Opera
- Musical theater
- Illusion
- Magic
- Mime
- Puppetry
- Spoken word
- Circus arts

Other options like magic, illusion, mime and puppetry etc., are good for you if you have the mind for it. Performing arts requires lots of practice and learning, so don't worry if you don't get it right initially. In a year or two, you will get the hang of it, or you can simply switch to some other great activity to spend some quality time.

Lucrative

According to the Bureau of Labor Statistics, managing a business is notoriously difficult, with over half of new companies failing within five years. However, you might be among the numerous retirees who are up for the challenge. According to the Ewing Marion Kauffman Foundation, new entrepreneurs aged 55 to 64 accounted for 26% of the population in 2017. Owning your own business might give you a feeling of purpose, the rush of a new challenge, and possibly some extra money for retirement. If you have always wanted to be your own boss, you can make a lot of the necessary preparations before you start, such as doing market research, creating a business plan, and selecting a location. Here are a few suggestions on where you may put your energy and time.:

Sublet Your Place

You can use Airbnb to rent out your excess room; you may make money hosting visitors from all over the world. It is currently present in 192 countries. For a day, week, or month, you can rent out a single room or your full house. There are other platforms as well to sublet your property. You can spread the word around in your local community and sublet a property you own.

Be An Entrepreneur

More and more people who are close to retirement age are choosing to pursue what is sometimes referred to as "encore entrepreneurship," which gives them the chance to finally transform their talents, experience, wisdom, and passion into a fruitful small business of their own. Retirees from the fastest growing group of entrepreneurs due to the promise of a sustained or a revitalized sense of purpose. You can create and market whatever good or service you want now that you aren't worried about making a living. Many retirees use their years of knowledge to work as independent consultants or advisors. You might also think about earning more money by:

- Taking care of a pet or a dog
- Setting up an online shop
- Providing babysitting services to local families
- Selling crafts through an Etsy shop
- Offering homemade cakes or jams at a farmers' market

Become A Consultant

Your professional insights, wisdom, and perspective are assets with significant value to individuals who need advice and consultancy. Opportunities for consultants can be found in almost every sector and range in size from macro to micro. As you get closer to retirement, working as a consultant may be a logical next step if you love what you do and want to leverage it on your own terms. With a diverse clientele, you can keep things fresh and have more flexibility over your schedule, who you want to deal with, and your fees. The secret is figuring out your specialization and how to sell your knowledge. It's fantastic to network with previous coworkers, clients, and contacts. You can set up an online consultancy platform, promote and advertise your services, get good reviews from clients you have already worked with and keep going.

Modeling

Yes, modeling is something that you can pursue even after your retirement. For people over 50, doing modeling is a new talk of the town, and you can also try it. It does not have to be fashion modeling; it can be product advertisement, promotion of services, magazines, or books. You can even sell your oven photographs on Shutterstock or other such websites to earn money. If you want to try modeling, then here is how to do it:

Be A Print Model:

First, decide whether you can dedicate your time to modeling. You must be honest about the time commitment if you truly want to achieve this. You will need to go to at least one audition per week, and a shoot can last up to two days. Take a decent headshot. Spend the cash and hire a professional for this. A headshot is the most crucial item you need to get started. Don't accept a friend's or an amateur's photo, either. You can use the photo for your Facebook page or that dating service you were considering joining, even if you don't land a modeling gig.

If you can, enroll in a commercial acting class and identify your "type." Despite the fact that we are discussing print modeling, taking a commercial acting class (again, for roughly $200 to $400) is a good method to feel at ease in front of the camera and learn how to follow directions. These modeling workshops are a great way to meet new people and can also help you overcome shyness and self-consciousness. You can discover your "type" for a print model role by taking commercial acting training. Are you a senior athlete who stays active? A warm and welcoming grandparent? A patient of medicine? You can learn that by taking those classes.

If you can register with a casting service. This may be extremely useful if you don't yet have a representative. Online casting agencies for print modeling and commercial acting are available in most major cities; they cost around $30 a month. If you can, get an agent. This process could take some time, and not everyone can pique an agent's interest. Because they don't get paid a commission if you don't get cast, the top agencies are quite picky. The best way to get to an agency is to mail a letter and headshot after looking for local print modeling agencies online. Many organizations also allow you to apply for representation online.

Outdoors

If you've always wanted to see the world, now is your chance! With no restrictions on your vacation time, you can travel the globe. Retirees are free to enjoy lengthy vacations and benefit from last-minute discounts. Many people take frequent vacations for activities like biking, golfing, shopping, or the arts. Some people only travel within their own country, while others venture abroad to discover locations like the Caribbean, Europe, and Latin America.

Rving

Rent or buy a trailer or RV and set out on the open road. Set a goal to explore every continent, travel, or visit every national park. A lifetime federal parks pass costs only $80 if you are over 62; in some states, the pass also offers significant savings on camping and boat launch fees. Become a host at a campground. Many RV parks and campgrounds provide free campsites and other perks in return for assistance with chores, including collecting fees, enforcing laws, and maintaining the grounds. Jobs in campground hosting are generally unpaid volunteer employment; however, some can offer a small pay and can run for a few weeks or a whole season. This may be an excellent approach to travel on a budget.

Camping

You are going to love camping if you are a nature lover. You can buy a camping kit, trekking gear and other accessories and get going with it. Autumn is the best season for nature therapy, whether through neighborhood walks or spending the night outside. Cooler temps bring wonderful sleeping conditions, fewer bothersome pests, fewer campers, and toasty campfires. Even if you haven't tented a camp in a while, you can take your camping gear to any of your favorite places, tag along with some friends or family members and camp!

Photography

We'll likely have a lot more time on our hands and a lot less rigidity after retirement. With this transformation, many of us start looking for new hobbies or life purposes. Photography is a passion that is pleasurable at any age. You may need photography to help you regain control of your health. It will keep your mind and body super-active and healthy and keep your mind in shape. You can buy a good camera with lenses and then start immediately.

Walking, running, and even hiking are frequent byproducts of a pastime in photography. Do you like taking pictures of the outdoors? Then you will need to travel to the locations of the landscapes, which typically requires some strenuous activity. Do you want to photograph people? You will then need to take a stroll through the neighborhood. Photography gets you to move around and find new inspirations, whether you prefer photographing nature, architecture, or other subjects. There are endless ways to do photography; the great benefit is that you can always sell your photographs or do a photo shoot for people.

Food photography

It is one great idea you can start working on from the comfort of your house. You will need a good resolution camera, a table, some accessories and your creative skills to get high-quality food pictures. You can sell those photos online for magazines, cookbooks etc.

Portrait Photography:

Portrait photography, sometimes referred to as portraiture, is a famous kind of photography that aims to capture the essence of a person or group. Thanks to how simple it is, you can set up a little studio in your home. Share your portfolio of images online to advertise your abilities. For various kinds of documents, people will come to your location to get their headshots done. Images may be close-ups, full-body poses, or candid shots. The right tone and emotion to get a good portrait picture by setting nice lighting and a backdrop. Portrait photography is used for a variety of purposes, the most frequent of which being family photos, engagement photos, senior portraits, and professional headshots. The finest portrait photographers enable their customers feel completely at ease, resulting in natural and calm facial expressions.

Photojournalism:

After retirement, you can try becoming a freelance photojournalist. Through the use of pictures, photojournalism tells the tale of a noteworthy (perhaps even historic) event or setting. Visit various events and hotspots, snap some excellent pictures, and send samples to periodicals or news organizations. You must be as impartial and authentic as can in your photojournalism, capturing candid situations instead of perfect images. Photojournalists typically go to organized events to get candid, unscripted shots. Regular publication of your work in periodicals and newspapers is possible.

Sea Life

Many sea-loving retirees love to live near the coast all year round. Why not go to the beach if you are retired or almost retired and seeking a new adventure? Retirement travelers are drawn to the sea for various reasons, including the stunning landscape, the clean, salty air, and a more laid-back lifestyle. Many places along the coastline encourage social connection, whether it be a family day at the beach, a walk along a cliff-top path, or an early morning swim. Coastal spaces often draw social engagement with others. Below is a list of things to do if you're lucky enough to be near the seaside:

Fishing

Why not go for an ocean fishing trip if you enjoy taking part in low-intensity exercise every time you visit the beach? You may enjoy getting up and diving in marine life while learning a new life skill by engaging in some deep-sea fishing. Going fishing by the ocean is a fantastic way to meet new people and form bonds around a common interest. A variety of ocean fishing businesses provide special programs for fishing, and you can join the expedition.

Taking A Walk

People of all ages can enjoy a leisurely walk along the shoreline as an excellent form of exercise and relaxation. Most folks would use their stroll to enjoy the lovely scenery and the calming sea wind with their loved ones. You can, however, follow the boardwalk all the way to the concession stalls and snack shacks at your neighborhood beach if you are feeling particularly daring. After that, you may have a full supper and engaging discussion with your family and friends while enjoying the stunning seaside scenery.

Scuba Diving

Scuba diving has many health advantages for anyone over the age of 60 who is moderately active and can benefit from them all. Scuba diving is a fantastic low-impact aerobic workout that provides all the cardiac advantages without the risk of joint damage. Blood flow is improved as a result of this. We can breathe underwater thanks to the Self-Contained Underwater Breathing Apparatus (SCUBA). The most important point to remember when scuba diving is to be safe. Never dive alone; resist the urge to acquire diving equipment and just jump in without getting trained. If you want to try scuba diving, visit several reputable diving schools and join them.

Surfing

Surfing offers various benefits to you, and you can try it as an adventurous adrenaline-kicking activity. There are numerous testimonials from people reporting that they become "one" with the water when they are surfing. More people claim that surfing is the foundation of their spirituality, religion, or way of life. So, what else should you watch out for while surfing?

Make sure to have fun, look after yourself, find some space, and be tranquil.

Mountain Life

Few aspiring retirees have enough money saved up to purchase a retirement house in the valleys surrounded by mountains or hills. If you are prepared to look past the most well-known ski areas, there are mountain communities that provide picturesque views and well-kept slopes at far lower costs. Your retirement money can be well invested in these mountainous locations because they offer affordable housing and outdoor leisure opportunities. Retirement in these reasonably priced mountain communities is a good option.

The following are some of the nice activities to do at these sort of places:

Hiking

Hiking is a wonderful way to experience nature. You can explore the wonders of nature at whichever speed suits you best when you are on your own two feet and simply carrying what you need for the day. And practically anyone may participate in it with a little thought and preparation. You can go out hiking with your partner or with friends. Make sure to suit up and take all the necessary tools and items to keep yourself safe.

Rafting

Whitewater rafting and rafting are outdoor recreational activities that are done by using a boat or an unsinkable raft. The degree of difficulty in rafting varies depending on the water's current where the sport is practiced. Although it may be done alone, it is more frequently done in groups, and managing the water requires strong teamwork. Whitewater rafting, river rafting, and canoeing are the most popular variations of this sport. Rafting is a team activity, so you can either join a group to carry it out or convince your family or friends to do it with you.

Gardening

Being outside may be really uplifting when the weather is good. After all, there are many pleasing sights, sounds, smells, and other sensory delights in the natural world. They enable you to experience the feeling of exploration or being part of something bigger than yourself. Growing your own flowers, vegetables, and fruits in your own backyard has to parallel; that you can enjoy nature while improving your mental health and ensuring sustainability. Here are some easy ways of gardening that you can try besides the traditional gardening techniques:

Raised-Bed Gardening

Raised gardens are outdoor, soil-based gardens similar to in-ground gardens. Because you need to build enclosures for your plants to reside in, this is the main difference. The box can be kinder to your back and can drain water more efficiently than an in-ground garden, although taking longer to construct. Raised gardens can be constructed using straw bales. You can install them in small places as well, for this type of gardening you don't need a special place, you can set them anywhere.

Container Gardening

Container gardening is a fantastic choice for novices when starting an indoor garden. This technique makes use of soil and entails growing plants in movable pots and boxes around your home. Your budding plants can be left outside in the sunshine. In other words, ensure your plant's container matches its dimensions. Your plant's container needs to expand as it does.

Hydroponic Gardening

If you are living in a house with no yard, you can set up a hydroponic garden on the roof or in any other suitable space. There are more affordable and simple ways to begin soilless gardening than the pricey and complex hydroponic gardening systems. Hydroponic gardens are perfect for someone who doesn't have much outdoor room to spare because they may be completely indoors. Nonetheless, hydroponic gardens still need regular upkeep and the purchase of fertilizers. Even if you buy a one-size-fits-all fertilizer, you should still keep an eye on what you're feeding each plant. The most adaptable gardening technique by far is hydroponic gardening, which allows you to grow any type of plant.

Spiritual

Spirituality is a way of feeding your soul, or any activity that satisfies your soul can be marked as spiritual. Spirituality, like religion, extends far beyond our ordinary lives and ultimately shapes how we view our place in the world. It involves a holistic strategy for achieving inner fulfillment and well-being. And as its name implies, spirituality centers on the human spirit and soul rather than the physical body. As we age, our need to connect to our souls becomes stronger. There are several everyday activities that we can try to be spiritual:

Be In Tune With Nature

It's incredible how spending time outdoors can soothe the soul. Simply step outside to listen to soothing noises like birdsong or crashing waves. You might also love spending time with animals, whether it be on a nearby farm or when a family member's dog or cat pays you a visit. Outdoor visual signals can also significantly impact a person's mental health. View picturesque scenery or a stunning display of fall color to experience it for yourself.

Enjoy Some Old Songs.

Music can significantly improve our well-being as we age, especially for people with memory disorders like dementia. Many dementia patients find that listening to certain hymns or songs can bring back happy, secure memories. Music may also help alleviate pain, according to a multitude of studies. Playing soothing music or hymns from a loved one's youth or early adulthood can aid in enhancing their comfort and spiritual well-being.

Meditation

It can be helpful to think back on pleasant experiences, especially for retirees who may suffer from despair. Keep a journal so you can write in it and reflect on your life. Another excellent method for reflection is meditation. To provide yourself with a time of uninterrupted introspection, you can join meditation sessions with cozy seats and soothing music.

Yoga

Doing yoga daily is another excellent way to connect to your soul and let your anxiety flow out of you. The philosophy behind yoga is that a person's physical body, ideas, feelings, and energy are all centered on the chakras. According to yogic gurus, their chakras influence people's emotional responses, wants, aversions, levels of confidence and fear, and even physical symptoms and repercussions. It causes physical, mental, or emotional imbalances that show symptoms like worry, sluggishness, or poor digestion when the energy in a chakra becomes blocked. The numerous physical poses used in yoga help release energy and balance out a chakra.

Charity

Charity is a nice way of giving back to the community you have lived in all your life. There are several forms of charities that you can go for. You can donate your money, time, services and other things to people. By giving out charity, you can feel more purposeful. Most retirees like to give their free time and expertise to do volunteer work for those in need. To become a volunteer, find out what kinds of organizations you are interested in, then see whether they could benefit from your skills. You can work at the following places to invest your time in others:

- Libraries: organize book collections and fundraising activities, or provide library resources to housebound adults.
- Hospices: Visit patients, read to them, or go for walks with them to show your support.
- Senior centers: Welcome visitors at the reception, run a computer lesson or assist in the kitchen.
- Theaters: Give out playbills and point them in the right direction so they can watch a show for free.
- Churches and other places of worship should plan and direct youth activities or community outreach projects.
- Museums: Guide visitors on tours and respond to their inquiries regarding the displays.
- Feed and groom animals, clean cages, or walk dogs at animal shelters.
- Food banks sift food products after receiving shipments and create packaging.

- Homes for veterans: Participate in creative projects, provide music for the residents, or accompany veterans to appointments.

Set Up A Charity Drive

Setting up a charity drive using your influence and efforts is a great initiative. You can set up a charity drive to help cancer patients, feed the homeless, help orphans, donate to people in war zones, or help people in rehabilitation centers. You can significantly impact your community by taking the helm of an initiative to assist others. Invite anybody who can help, including members of your family, friends, club, past coworkers, and others. To find out what is most needed, speak with nearby charities. You can think about raising money for a special needs organization, assembling presents for sick kids, or providing clothing for catastrophe victims.

Arts And Crafts

If you are a creative soul who finds pleasure in doing artwork, finding some suitable arts and crafts activity is a good hobby. These kinds of imaginative leisure activities are fantastic for people of all ages. Making an art piece instills a person's hope and a sense of possibility. Your sense of success is heightened and you feel more fulfilled when you create a masterpiece. Though there are endless ways to express your inner creativity, here are a few options that you can try:

Ceramics

Learning to produce ceramic plates, vases, bowls, and other forms of pottery may be done for a low cost. The typical price to learn this craft in a class is between $20 and $40. You can set up a little pottery shop at home to get started. Being able to produce beautiful and functional ceramic products requires time and effort. To construct any sculpture, you'll need a potters wheel, glazes, clay tools, and a kiln. It could take a few days to finish a small project, like producing a plate, mug, or bowl, before it can be used.

Create Miniature Art

Miniatures demand a lot of patience, but they are a soothing way to relieve stress because they need the use of common household supplies like paint and tweezers to piece together fragile models. Expect to be absorbed for a few hours or days, making model ships in bottles, town dioramas, or recreations of historical characters if you can also sell your miniatures online.

You may also attempt these other kinds of arts and crafts:

- Painting
- Sketching/drawing
- Ceramics
- Mosaics
- Woodcraft
- Polymer clay modeling
- Papercraft
- Beading
- Knitting
- Crocheting
- Embroidery
- Quilt making
- Card making
- Jewelry making

Family

We all plan to give time to the family while thinking about retirement. Without becoming an over-annoying and over-involved senior in the house, there are several ways in which you can enjoy some quality time with your family. Finding the correct balance is all you need to do when it comes to spending time in the house Listed here is a listing of family outings that you must take into account:

Revamp Your House

Why not make improvements to your home that will make it more attractive, practical, or secure? You could put up a fence, turn a kid's old room into a home office or gym, repaint your walls, cabinets, or other home furnishings, or improve your house's curb appeal with inexpensive upgrades like shutters and window boxes or solar lighting.

Take Care Of Your Grandchildren

If you have grandchildren, then spending time with them while doing all their favorite activities is a fulfilling family activity. You can take your little grandkids cycling or for a walk in the park. It enables substantial cost savings on child care. Make sure you want to commit to this before offering to watch your grandchildren. It depends on the retirement goals you have set for yourself. For instance, you probably won't be able to commit to caring for your grandchildren on a regular basis if you start traveling for a longer period of time. If you don't have enough time to watch children every week, you might volunteer to be a "babysitting safety net" so that your kids can ask you to watch them if no one else is available.

Retire Like A Millennial

Retire like a millennial? What does that even mean?

Well, several studies have suggested that the millennial's approach to retirement is altogether different from their predecessors- Generation X. In retirement, Millennials are more likely to value travel than housing. For them, the most important thing in life is being able to spend their money as they see fit, rather than worrying about their finances. More than conventional retirement pastimes, they are drawn to the freedom and novel experiences. They are less concerned about having a certain amount saved for retirement. But they consider retirement savings as an ongoing process, and they like to be able to follow their interests even after they stop working. They are more into socializing and living a life of freedom, and if you want to retire like millennials, then here are some activities that you can go for:

Organize Events And Other Social Occasions

Making new friends and acquaintances can be a great way to add more enjoyment to your life. That is especially true if you get to chat about other topics that interest you or reflect on the past. In fact, engaging in a stimulating conversation may do more to improve your disposition and attitude than anything else on this list. Therefore, don't be afraid to go to other people's parties or join clubs. Also, think about organizing a few of your own events. You can organize gatherings on a variety of subjects, including:

- Murder mystery
- Casino night
- Trivia night
- Masquerade ball

- Mexican fiesta
- The 1920s, 1950s, and 1960s, etc.
- Arabian nights
- Mardi Gras
- Pirates
- Hawaiian luau
- Jungle bash
- The Oscars
- Formal tea
- Secret Santa
- Ugly sweaters night
- Backyard BBQ parties

Summer is one of my favorite seasons of the year, and I consider myself to be a grill master. I get to roll out my barbecue and make use of it almost every night of the week. But as much as I like grilling up a couple of nice Ribeyes for my family, having guests over for a backyard barbeque is much more enjoyable. Keeping things informal is essential to a pleasant BBQ. Don't overdo it with the menu; concentrate on a few tried-and-true dishes. Consider quality above quantity. Choose one or two meaty dishes (steaks, hamburgers, or sausages are good choices) and a simple vegetarian dish (roasted veggie skewers are always a win). Provide a few salads and condiments, or just serve corn on the cob, a barbecue staple. You can plan a bonfire night with music and games with your friends and loved ones.

Play Games

Card games and board games are great ways to interact with others while enjoying the fun challenges of friendly competition. Solving puzzles might help you develop your mental skills and feel like you've made progress. You can invite friends over and set up a match of the following games:

Monopoly

Monopoly is a great board game, and you can buy a set for yourself to play with your friends and partner. You can set up matches and tournaments to make it interesting.

Chess

Chess is a strategy game; thus, it demands a lot of mental Sharpness. The game encourages players to use different regions of their brains to plan, analyze, and solve problems. Your brain works really hard when you play chess frequently!

There are many other games which you can now play offline and online using the internet:

- Uno
- Word search puzzles
- Scrabble
- Rummy
- Pictionary
- Yahtzee
- Bingo
- Poker
- Checkers
- Chinese checkers
- Crazy Eights
- Monopoly
- Backgammon
- Crossword puzzles
- Cribbage
- Go Fish
- Bridge
- Mahjong
- Canasta
- Dominoes
- Solitaire
- Jigsaw puzzles

Conclusion

Knowing how an incredible life you can spend after retirement is a great relief; it keeps you motivated, and often people pursue their lifelong passion or dream after retirement. Our work life is often influenced by the financial pressures we face at that age, but once you get out of all those responsibilities and pressures, you will start seeing life differently, and you will want to cherish every little moment that you have with your family, your friends and yourself.

My post-retirement life has been a journey of self-exploration, and every other day I learn a new thing that makes this whole experience so fulfilling.

With all those ideas that I have shared in this comprehensive guide, you can also experience the same. Set your finances straight, manage your accounts and then make a bucket list of your own. Start with something plain and simple from the fun activities I have listed. You can set your goals for a week or a month, or even for a year; there is no pressure- it is never too late to pursue what you love to do.

Have a happy retirement!

Printed in Great Britain
by Amazon